A CITIZEN

UNITED STATES

BY LORRAINE SINTETOS

PEARSON

Scott Foresman

Editorial Offices: Glenview, Illinois • Parsippany, New Jersey • New York, New York

Sales Offices: Needham, Massachusetts • Duluth, Georgia • Glenview, Illinois
Coppell, Texas • Ontario, California • Mesa, Arizona

1. Being a Citizen

"He is a United States citizen." "Be a good citizen." Compare these two statements. Ask yourself if the word *citizen* means the same thing in each sentence.

The word *citizen* has different meanings. In the first sentence, the word has a legal meaning. A United States citizen is a citizen by law. In the second sentence it has a social meaning. Here, *citizen* means "a member of a group." As you read this book, you will learn more about each meaning.

2. What Makes You a United States Citizen?

There are three ways to become a United States citizen. One way is to be born in the United States.

You can also be born to parents who are United States citizens. In this case where you are born is not important. As long as one of your parents is a citizen of the United States, you are also a citizen.

The third way is to study to become a citizen. Many of the thousands of **immigrants** who come here each year do just that. They learn about the history of the United States. They learn about how the government works. They also learn about the rights shared by citizens of the United States.

Some immigrants come here with the plan of staying a short time and then going home. They stay as long as needed to go to school or to work. A large number of immigrants, however, want the **opportunity** to become citizens with the rights that only citizens have. They want the right to vote and even to run for office. These people can become naturalized citizens by meeting the requirements on the chart below.

YOU MUST BE EIGHTEEN YEARS OLD OR OLDER.

YOU MUST HAVE LIVED IN THE UNITED STATES
FOR AT LEAST FIVE YEARS.

YOU MUST BE ABLE TO READ, SPEAK, AND WRITE ENGLISH.

YOU MUST KNOW ABOUT UNITED STATES HISTORY
AND GOVERNMENT.

★ ★ ★ ★ ★ ★ ★ ★ ★

These are some requirements for becoming a naturalized citizen.

To become United States citizens, immigrants must take a written test. The one hundred questions test knowledge of United States history and government.

Stories from our history help people understand us. They show how we got our rights and freedoms. Learning about the past shows what is important.

Knowing about our government is helpful. To fully participate in the government, citizens need to understand how our government works and how it protects our freedoms. Citizens also need to know certain **customs** of this country.

3. Responsibilities Go with Rights

Our country guarantees many rights to its citizens. We are free to say or write what we think. We have the right to know what our government is doing. Each of us has the right to be treated fairly.

Our government also provides many of the services we need. It runs schools, libraries, parks, and police and fire stations. It manages our mail service and provides us with clean water.

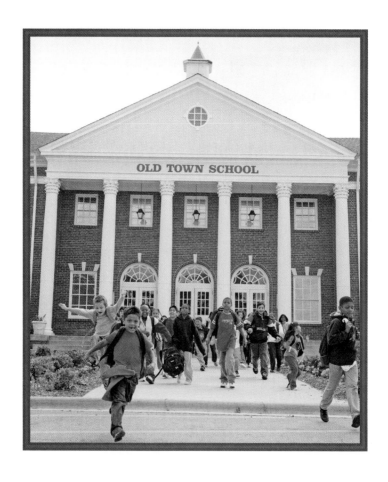

One of our major rights is the right to choose our leaders by voting. Once a citizen is eighteen years old, he or she has the right to vote.

With the right to vote comes the responsibility of voting wisely. At election time we should read the newspapers and watch TV carefully to learn about our leaders. We should ask who will help make laws that are good for the United States.

Another one of our responsibilities is paying taxes to the government. You might pay taxes when you buy something because a sales tax is added to your bill. There are many different kinds of taxes. The government uses tax money to provide services to its citizens.

We have a responsibility to obey laws. Many laws are made to protect us. Some laws make sure we are treated fairly and help us live together. Other laws protect our safety and health.

Traffic laws help prevent accidents. They tell us how to ride or drive safely. Some health laws set standards for how to prepare food and treat water so that they are clean and safe.

Some laws make sure that our country will be a good place to live. You must attend school so that you will learn to read, write, and think clearly. This will help you and your classmates become good citizens and smart voters when you are adults. Some of you may even become leaders in your **community**.

4. Everyone Can Be a Good Citizen

Think about the social meaning of *citizen*. It means "someone who lives in a community." When people live close together, they are all citizens of that community. With this meaning a citizen can even be a visitor from another country.

A community has a lot to offer its citizens. Its buses, shops, schools, and parks are there for everyone to use. Trash may be picked up and mail may be delivered. Snow and leaves may be removed from a community's streets. When you are older, a community can provide work for you. Your community takes care of many of your needs and will continue to do so for your entire life.

To give back to the community, people try to be good citizens. Being a good citizen is not hard if you remember to think of others' needs. Before you act or speak, stop to think about the effect of your actions or words on others.

You already know a number of ways to be a good citizen.
- Treat other people fairly.
- Be polite.
- Share what you have.
- Take turns.
- Do not take or damage another's property.
- Solve problems by talking.

5. Improving Your Community

If you are on a street where trash blows across the sidewalk and fills the gutter, would you look around and feel happy? Garbage is not a pretty sight. Litter makes it look as if people do not care about their community.

Keeping streets clean is one way to be a good citizen and show pride in your community. It shows respect for your neighbors.

Some communities have clean-up days. People work together to throw away trash. Buildings are fixed and painted. Flowers are planted. Citizens work together to improve their community.

We are all citizens of the world. We take pride in how we care for Earth. We should think about the effects of our actions years from now. We have a responsibility to the people who will live after us. We owe it to them to keep our air and water clean. We can try to leave Earth better than it is.

You can do your part by riding your bike or walking to where you want to go. Each time a car gets on the road, it produces gases that dirty the air and make it harder to breathe. Help keep our water clean by not throwing trash into rivers and lakes. **Recycle** as much as you can.

   Good citizens are careful not to use up Earth's
natural resources. A natural resource helps us
meet our needs. A resource is something such as
trees, oil, and minerals. Stop to think of some ways
we use each of these things. We do not have an
endless supply of them.

   Each time you buy something new, you use up
the resources that went into making it. If fewer
people buy products, fewer products will be made.
Make trades or share with friends. Take good care
of what you own so you will not need to replace it.

6. Making a Difference

Good citizens can become volunteers to help other people in their community. Volunteers work without being paid.

You do not have to be an adult to be a volunteer. You can cheer up older people in nursing homes or help younger children with their homework. You can pick up litter in a nearby park. In some towns there are jobs at libraries for young people in the summer. There are many ways for you to help in your community!

Many of us have the same hopes for our lives. We want to have our needs met and to live peacefully and safely. We want to be treated fairly and enjoy our freedom.

We can help these things happen by being good citizens. This means being thoughtful of others and living in an unselfish way.

Each time you make your community a bit better through your actions, you make the world a bit better too.

Glossary

citizen a member of a community

community a place where people live, work, and have fun together

custom a way of doing things

immigrant a person who moves into a country to live there

natural resource useful material that comes from the Earth

opportunity a chance for something better to happen

recycle to use something again